THE LEAST WE CAN DO

INDEPENDENT BOOKSTORE DAY 2021

The Least We Can Do

*White Supremacy, Free Speech,
and Independent Bookstores*

Josh Cook

BIBLIOASIS
Windsor, Ontario

1.

Apology

WHEN SEAN SPICER was given prime billing at BookExpo America and Milo Yiannopoulos tried to publish a book with Simon & Schuster, I churned out forty pages of text about free speech, White supremacy, and independent bookstores over the next several months, returning to it now and then as a salve or outlet for my frustration and then just … let it sit. I should have written something even earlier, after I had been in bookselling for ten years and watched Republicans and conservatives profiting—in terms of money and power—off the racist backlash to the Obama administration. Someone should have written something even earlier, as we watched the Bush administration start two endless wars, institute torture as an official American practice, and completely remake American society after the trauma of 9/11. Someone should have written something when Rush Limbaugh's first book was published, before the reactionary racism of right-wing talk shows became fully mainstream. Like so many White, liberal Americans, I thought the gains made during the Civil Rights Movement were secure and that even if there was still a long way to go towards true social and racial justice, at least we weren't sliding back. It's embarrassing. Only the thinnest veils were thrown over the racism of the war on drugs, criminal justice reform, and welfare reform. Even after the Tea Party rose to power almost entirely through the White grievance and racism stoked by Fox News. Even after the Republican Party formally embraced this radical version of themselves. I did not see a resurgent threat and I did not see my complicity in that resurgence.

At most, I was an active participant in a conversation with the Porter Square Books managers group about our relationship to books written by and/or supporting contemporary right-wing, conservative, and/or Republican authors, with some of us arguing that we needed to dramatically change that relationship, and others arguing that the current relationship is correct. Parts of that conversation will appear throughout this essay. But as the Trump administration, Fox News, and Republican politicians enacted more and more racist and destructive policies, we never re-examined that compromise. It just never seemed like the right time. There were always more pressing problems. Once the pandemic hit, we never felt like we had the emotional reserves for that difficult conversation. And I didn't force it. I expressed myself on Twitter and in informal conversations, but I never truly pushed for a formal re-examination of what books we should allow on our platforms, what ideas we want to give space to, and what people we want to be a revenue stream for.

Money is power. The more money you have, the more time you can spend advancing your cause, the more people you can hire to help advance your cause, the more you can donate to other people and organizations advancing your cause. If you have money, you can pay lobbyists, create fake and biased studies to support your ideologies, make misleading advertisements, hire lawyers to litigate cases you think will advance your cause, pay troll farms to harass your opponents on social media. If you can't convince people of your ideas, but you have enough money, you can get those ideas reflected in government policy anyway.

If you have published a book, people will listen to what you say, at least more than they will if you haven't. If people see your book at a bookstore, they will conclude that the book world believes your ideas are worth reading. Whether they agree with your ideas or not, the fact of a traditionally published book tells readers some basic level of value or legitimacy has been reached. Furthermore, publishing a book unlocks other platforms for your ideas: book reviews, media appearances, events, and other publicity. You'll get the chance to point people to your website and social media. If you're lucky, or have some specific supports, you'll even make money.

Donald Trump was president, in part, because the media, publishers, bookstores, book reviewers, readers, and everyone with power and influence in books decided it was okay to sell books by Rush Limbaugh, Bill O'Reilly, Ann Coulter, Laura Ingraham, Michael Savage, Sean Hannity, Tucker Carlson, and all the other right-wing pundits and politicians, monetizing and legitimizing the White supremacist ideas they expressed and providing a platform for those ideas to reach more people. Donald Trump was president because we did not take responsibility for our own decisions. Donald Trump was president because we did nothing when con artists monetized White grievance, White fear, and White supremacy. Most of us took some of that money. Some of us took a lot of that money. Donald

Trump was president because the conservative movement over the last thirty years broke our political media's bullshit detector. Donald Trump was president because people like Newt Gingrich, Paul Ryan, Mike Pence, Ted Cruz, and, well, Donald Trump himself were taken seriously, as if they were honestly participating in American political discourse. Donald Trump was president because publishers and bookstores showed readers that we believed those people and ideas deserved to be taken seriously.

Whatever we do going forward, we can no longer pretend that we are innocent. Donald Trump put children in cages. We can no longer act as though book sales do not have ethical and moral components. Donald Trump sabotaged the national response to COVID-19, killing hundreds of thousands of people. We cannot pretend that it does not matter who we help make money. A Confederate flag was waved in the Capitol building during a violent insurrection that killed six people. We cannot pretend that we don't have some responsibility over what ideas are discussed in public discourse.

Like many industries and institutions, booksellers have done a lot of work in the last few years in response to the Trump administration, the Black Lives Matter Movement, the #MeToo movement, and other events and forces for social change in our society. We've formed committees, hosted panels, and held training sessions and though all of that is important, I have almost never seen booksellers grapple directly with the economic, social, and moral consequences of selling books by White supremacists, fascists, misogynists, and other believers in objectively dangerous ideologies. Though I will offer some specific strategies, I hope this piece acts as the start of a more sustained conversation about the relationship between bookselling, politics, and free speech. Furthermore, free speech is a concept with ragged edges and many of the decisions we make about what speech is protected or not, what speech is appropriate for what spaces, what speech should be amplified on which platforms, require nuance and context to be made. Since I can't provide that nuance and context for everything, I'm going to focus on speech by Republicans with actual political power and Fox News and conservative pundits with significant influence over politics and policy.

I apologize for waiting this long to take this small step within my industry. I apologize for not listening to what many, many people had tried to tell me and all of White America about the threat to our country. I apologize for prioritizing avoiding interpersonal conflict with friends, family, and colleagues over confronting a persistent and deadly threat. I don't know if what I've written here will make a big difference. I don't know if independent bookstores have enough power to make a big difference in the fight against White supremacy, other supremacist ideologies, and fascism in America. But we have some power. And if we don't fight, we can't win.

To Some, This is Already a Civil War

THE CURRENT STATE of American governance is not politics as usual. It isn't even the usual "let's find a way to be racist that isn't quite as bad" of most of American legislative politics. It isn't just "partisan bickering" or "both sides have some good ideas and some bad ideas." You may be insulated from the violence surging through our country. You may not spend time in radical right-wing corners of the internet. You may not see the recruiting efforts, the merchandise, the planning, the infiltration of our law enforcement and military by organized White supremacists, but all of that is happening. Some people in this country believe we are in a Civil War, in the exact same way that some people believe the apocalypse is imminent, and they are acting like it.

It seems almost ... silly to spend time on this after the violent insurrection on January 6, 2021, but apparently even pipe bombs placed around D.C., men in military gear with zip cuffs and perhaps even assassination plans, evidence of coordination with members of Congress, and six people dead is not enough to convince everyone that we are in an armed and violent conflict. In fact, as I write this, Republicans in Congress are acting as if the insurrection wasn't the violent assault we all watched on national television, but a peaceful protest. Some Republicans are just moving on, some are denying various aspects of it, some are spreading misinformation and conspiracy theories about it and none of the Republican politicians with any kind of power (to date) have suffered any consequences whatsoever. But this is not something that will just pass. It was never something that would just pass. This is not something that will get sorted out in Congressional committees. This was never something that would get sorted out in Congressional committees. This is not something that will get hashed out in the marketplace of ideas. This was never something that would get hashed out in the marketplace of ideas. And this won't end with the Trump administration, no matter what eventually happens (or does not happen) to Donald Trump himself, just like it didn't end with the Nixon administration, the Reagan administration, or the two Bush administrations.

The complicity of American publishing and bookselling with White supremacy is not the most powerful force
supporting and sustaining White supremacy in America.
It's probably a minor one. And whatever antiracist and antifascist actions we take within our industry will also be
relatively minor compared to actions taken by other institutions and industries. But we should take them, nonethe-
less. There are no minor actions in a civil war.

2.

There Are No Free Speech Absolutists

THE FIRST TIME I heard the term "free speech absolutist" was in a conversation with another bookseller several
years ago about the American Booksellers Association's
new code of conduct for events and conferences. This
other bookseller's concern was that people would be so
afraid of saying something that could be considered a
violation of the code of conduct that free speech would
be curtailed. Booksellers would choose to remain silent,
rather than risk whatever punishments were in the code.
I understand being concerned with making clear distinctions between speech that is "offensive" and speech that is
"harassing" or between speech that makes people "uncomfortable" and speech that makes people "unsafe," but the
term "free speech absolutism" doesn't actually interact
with those distinctions. Even when used as kind of short-
hand for giving the benefit of the doubt to allowing rather
than restricting speech, the term obfuscates the debate by
shutting down the nuance around these issues.

I cannot call you up in the middle of the night and tell you I'm going to murder you. I cannot send an email to your boss that claims you were convicted of cruelty to animals. If I am a pharmaceutical company, I cannot say my new drug cures cancer if it doesn't cure cancer. I cannot tell you that I'm a doctor or lawyer or police officer if I am not. I cannot tell the IRS I made no money when, in fact, I made a lot of money. (Well, I can, but I have to speak a very specific language.) I can't say "fuck" on certain media at certain times of day, I can't use TV advertising to try to convince children to smoke, and, of course, I can't shout "Fire!" in a crowded theater. There has never been, there will never be, and no one has ever actually argued for, absolute freedom of speech.

Though some people, like the bookseller I was talking with, certainly use the term in good faith and it certainly sounds like a principled idea, most of the time arguments for "absolute freedom of speech" aren't actually used to advance an idea or work towards the truth. Rather, they are designed to shift the debate away from the ideas themselves while creating space to occupy on a platform. It is, essentially, a kind of rhetorical jiu jitsu that creates publicity and recruitment opportunities, obscures the terms of the discussion, and shifts the focus away from problematic or difficult-to-defend ideas to vaguer notions of free speech. If there was any doubt, any ambiguity, any space to learn something about personal expression and its relationship to society, it might be worth our time to seriously engage with arguments that include versions of the phrase "free speech absolutist," but there isn't, so we don't.

Progress Towards Better Ideas

RATHER THAN THINKING of our discourse as "the market-place of ideas," I think of it as society's scientific method: people offer ideas (trial) and the use, meaning, and verac-ity of the ideas are examined until a flaw is revealed or a different idea is agreed to be better (error). As with any scientific endeavor, the more trials we have, the more truths we can discover. Protecting free speech allows for the greatest volume of these intellectual trials and errors.

But not all ideas or expressions are actual intellectual trials. Take, for example, the sentence "Cheetahs are a type of tree." This is, obviously, not true. But not only is it not true, it also doesn't help discover any truth. Everyone knows cheetahs are not trees and re-proving the fact that cheetahs aren't trees doesn't help produce some other truth.

Take a more reasonable example from the debate around the Affordable Care Act, the signature legislation from Barack Obama's first term as president. Very broadly, the Affordable Care Act's goal was to lower healthcare costs through a number of different mechanisms while leaving it based in private health insurance. It was modeled direct-ly on the Massachusetts health care program signed into law by Republican governor Mitt Romney. There was a lot of nonsense in the debate around the ACA, but the most nonsensical was the accusation that it created "death pan-els," essentially euthanasia bureaucrats who would decide whether or not your grandma would get the healthcare she needed. The substance from which this lie was drawn is the provision that allows for Medicare to cover optional appointments dealing with living wills and other end-of-life care issues. If you can't see how coverage of optional counseling sessions (which absolutely could result in a patient deciding "Don't you dare unplug me!") could become death panels … well … exactly. But the idea nevertheless gained traction, boosted by the likes of Sarah Palin and former lieutenant governor of New York Betsy McCaughey, and marred the debate long after it was debunked. It was rated "Pants on Fire" pretty much every time it was repeated and named the Lie of the Year by PolitiFact.

By lying about "death panels" right-wing critics of the Affordable Care Act sabotaged the discourse around it. Instead of debating things like whether there was enough funding allotted for the roll out of the technology or exploring other improvements to the actual bill, the discourse wasted time and energy on a problem that did not exist. (I would argue that most of that was tactical rather than earnest, as it is a lot easier to get people to oppose the ACA because "Euthanasia is bad" than it is because "people should have their financial lives ruined because they cannot afford to pay their medical bills.") To return to my extended metaphor, the idea that the ACA created panels of bureaucrats that could deny life-saving care to the elderly was not an actual intellectual trial from which other truth could be learned, and just like proving cheetahs are not trees, we learned nothing from proving the ACA did not have "death panels." To be clear, I'm not arguing that people who claimed the ACA was out to murder grandma should have been thrown in jail for expressing that opinion; I'm saying that we shouldn't have given them platforms to express that idea, that if they wrangled a platform anyway they should have been shut down once they started to express that idea, and that depending on who they were, what their jobs were, and how much power they had, they should have suffered professional consequences for their lies, especially if they kept saying it after it was debunked.

Is Compromise Possible Between Opposing Ideas?

MOST OF THE time, we have to act even when we haven't reached consensus about an action, idea, or policy. In those cases, we must find compromise between the proposed ideas in order to move forward with whatever we are doing. Just as we need as many honest ideas as possible for all those trials, we need as many honest ideas as possible from which to explore compromise. For example, "the rich should pay no taxes," is a terrible idea, but we can at least imagine compromises between it and the idea "the rich should pay taxes commensurate with the benefits they have received from society."

But compromise isn't possible with some ideas. What would represent a compromise between the ideas "Cheetahs are a type of tree" and "No, they're not, you fucking weirdo?" Or perhaps, "I would like to burn your house down," and "Please don't burn my house down?" Is a half-burned house really a compromise? If it is possible to find some kind of compromise between the expressed idea and its opposite then it will probably also contribute to that whole society's scientific method thing. But if it's not, what work does the idea do? And if the idea does no work, why would you have an obligation to include it on your platform?

Supremacist Ideas and the Possibility of Compromise

AS OTHERS HAVE eloquently pointed out, there is no

compromise between "Black people are human beings" and "Black people are not human beings." And we know this, not just because of obvious logic, but because the vast majority of America's social and economic problems and injustices are rooted in trying to create a compromise between "Black people are human beings" and "Black people are not human beings." Can you imagine looking someone in the eye and telling them they need to believe what they are watching is a "debate" or "free exchange of ideas" if one of the possible conclusions is "You are not human?" Furthermore, the process that created this "compromise" is much less like actual compromise and much more like appeasement. To many (to most), this isn't a conversation. It's a conflict. To others, this isn't a debate. It is still a war.

Supremacist ideas, in the form of White supremacy, in the form of misogyny, in the form of xenophobia, are inherently antithetical to compromise. In a White supremacist society, White people do not have to compromise with non-White people, regardless of the issues, ideas, policies, and potential actions. In a misogynist society, men don't need to compromise with women. In a xenophobic society, you don't have to compromise with someone born in a different country. The alt-right, White supremacists, incels, fascists, and a whole lot of people who would consider themselves (and are considered) to be mainstream Republicans don't actually believe in compromise; they believe in getting what they want, however they can.

Whatever is Happening Isn't Basketball

IMAGINE IF A basketball player stopped dribbling and just ran with the ball and dunked it. Now, imagine if the two points counted. Maybe the player is ashamed and never does it again. Maybe that's the end of it. Or maybe the player does it again and gets away with it again. It's a lot easier to score if you don't have to dribble. (Joke about how James Harden doesn't have to dribble.) So more players stop dribbling. Maybe some still do. Maybe a lot still do for a whole host of reasons but those who dribble lose. So now some players never dribble, some dribble every now and then, some dribble most of the time, and some still dribble all the time like they're supposed to. Something is happening on basketball courts, but it's not basketball. That is the state of American discourse. Very broadly, one team is still mostly playing basketball, while the other team just picks up the ball and runs.

There are problems with using sports, or any kind of competition, as a metaphor for the state of discourse because, in theory, discourse should not be a competition. Despite all of our differences and disagreements, everyone involved in our discourse *should* have the same goal; to work towards policies that make the world better. Even though we differ on how to make that happen, even though we differ on what constitutes "better," the "winner" or "loser" of the debate is irrelevant to the solution the debate produced.

Over the course of American history various groups, identities, and ideologies have treated discourse as a competition, as something that can be won or lost. The thing about making winning your only goal, is, well, you tend to win. Not all the time, of course, but way more than you would have if your only goal had been to play the best basketball you could. If political representation was based on which party would enact the policies most Americans support, Democrats would have been in power at almost every level of government for a quarter of a century or more. So, more and more Republicans have played only to win. When they stopped being able to convince people to vote for them, they stopped trying to convince people, instead shifting their focus to turning out their base by incorporating whatever right-wing nonsense was most motivating at the time and leveraging specific wedge issues (same sex marriage, gun control, abortion) that inspired those voters, then moving on to the next when either the issue was resolved or the voters' focuses changed. (Notice how little we hear about gay marriage now. Notice how once gay marriage was made legal by the Supreme Court, the greatest threat to American society was suddenly transgender rights.) As the cynical techniques worked, the techniques got more cynical. When the information didn't support Republican goals, they spread misinformation. When their actions were questioned they used "whattaboutism" rather than actually defending those actions. They prevented the passage of or refused to support any policy that could be considered a win for the Democrats, even if, like the ACA, that win included plenty of Republican policies and priorities. They gerrymandered districts at an unprecedented level so they could maintain legislative control whether more people voted for them or not. When the Voting Rights Act was gutted, they added enhanced voter suppression to their arsenal, specifically tailoring voting laws to discourage likely Democratic voters.

They still use the gestures and language of rational debate and they certainly argue that their opponents have an obligation to convince them of absolutely everything (even things they may have previously agreed with), but the vast majority of new voters they have gained over the last few years seem to have gotten there through indoctrination by Fox News and the right-wing internet.

What is the value of having ideas from Republicans in your stores if the authors of those ideas aren't actually looking to convince anyone their ideas are correct?

Using the Court to Do Anything But Play Basketball

OUTSIDE OF CONGRESSIONAL politics we saw another technique, especially after the advent of the internet. Radical right-wing groups hijacked the mechanisms of discourse not to actually engage in those debates but to simply occupy that space, essentially as a publicity technique. Because the ragged edges of free speech require nuanced debate to navigate, because very broadly most people support free speech, and because as a culture Americans identify "free speech" as a fundamental value, positioning yourself in that ongoing debate about what types of speech have the right or privilege to happen in what types of spaces is an easy way to occupy space in a discourse whether that discourse has anything to do with free speech and whether your point about free speech does any productive work in the discourse. This is why "cancel culture" is such a common talking point from the right. (Which was of course preceded by "political correctness.") It allows them to reframe a debate about sexual harassment in professional settings, or antisemitism, or how an estate wants to manage an artist's past use of racist imagery, away from those issues, while, at the same time, maintaining their participation in the discussion around those issues.

To return to our basketball court: imagine if teams

started putting out extra players who just ... stood there with websites on their jerseys. Every now and then maybe they wave at the ball or take a step or two in the direction of the play, but they really just spend most of their time arguing with the ref that they should be allowed to be there. Once again, we find ourselves with something happening in the space, but it's not really a basketball game.

Popper's Paradox of Tolerance.

KARL POPPER'S PARADOX of tolerance, from *The Open Society and its Enemies*, is a relatively simple idea (especially in the world of paradoxes): if you allow every voice into a space, with no moderation, eventually intolerant voices will make it an intolerant space, resorting to violence if they need to in order to control the space. Whether we're talking about Weimar Germany or the punk rock and hardcore music scenes, when you tolerate White supremacists in your space, your space becomes a White supremacist space. "Unlimited tolerance must lead to the disappearance of tolerance. If we extend unlimited tolerance," Popper argued, "even to those who are intolerant, if we are not prepared to defend a tolerant society against the onslaught of the intolerant, then the tolerant will be destroyed, and tolerance with them." We're actually watching experiments in low-moderation space in real time on social media. Many people, especially women and even more especially women of color, do not express themselves on Twitter because when they do, Twitter allows their timelines to be flooded with death and rape threats, threats against their families and children, and messages that would get someone fired or arrested in virtually any other context. A death threat cannot be answered with rational debate. As Popper says, "it may easily turn out that [the intolerant] are not prepared to meet us on the level of rational argument, but begin by denouncing all argument; they may forbid their followers to listen to rational argument, because it is deceptive, and teach them to answer arguments by the use of their fists or pistols." To put this another way, conservatives and other right-wing thinkers, pundits, and politicians frequently use harassment to stifle the free speech of other people on social media. "We should therefore claim, in the name of tolerance, the right not to tolerate the intolerant." Twitter would actually have much more open discourse and be a much more tolerant space if it actually enforced its own terms of service and refused to tolerate intolerance.

I can already hear someone arguing that no one needs to be on Twitter (or any other social media) and though that is sort of true (though it conveniently ignores how many jobs, especially in the book industry, require a social media presence) it's also kind of my point. Intolerant acts drive people away and eventually you end up with a purely intolerant space.

Back to the Lab

TO CIRCLE BACK to the language of science: lies, misinformation, bad faith arguments, and expressions that negate the expression of others are like tampering with lab results. We cannot find a cure for cancer if someone mislabels the samples, lies about the results, refuses to change their conclusions after those conclusions have been shown incorrect, or in any other way obscures or diminishes the results of the testing. The discourse around finding a cure for cancer is only productive if everyone involved is primarily concerned with finding a cure for cancer and is willing to be open and honest with their tests and arguments and open to being critiqued and shown wrong in their efforts. Likewise, the discourse around national policy is only productive if everyone involved in that discourse is committed to finding the best national policy rather than having their guy win. Just as science doesn't work if those with power over its application do not believe in science, democracy, in whatever form it takes, doesn't work if a critical mass of those participating in the dialogue do not believe in democracy.

Stamped from the Beginning

EVERY NOW AND then you read a book and something mysterious snaps into focus. I had always wondered why contemporary Republicans could act like increasing the federal deficit was the single worst sin an administration could commit when Democrats wanted to spend money on social programs yet they themselves increase the deficit all the time with tax breaks, military spending, and wars when they are in power. In *Stamped from the Beginning: The Definitive History of Racist Ideas in America*, Dr Ibram X Kendi shows that racist policies and practices preceded racist ideas and ideologies. The ideas were designed to justify slavery, rather than slavery growing out of racist ideas. Because the job of these ideas is to support a specific policy, they aren't held to the same standards as other ideas. They don't need to be consistent over time. They don't need to incorporate agreed upon fact. They don't need to be internally consistent. They can even include facets that are mutually exclusive.

The Three-Fifths Compromise is a perfect example of the flexible logic of racist ideas. Under the compromise, three-fifths of a state's slave population would count towards the state's total population, increasing the number of representatives the state would have in the House of Representatives. That makes no sense. If slaves are property rather than human beings, why should their number count towards political power? Elbridge Gerry of Massachusetts asked why should "blacks, who were property in the South," count toward representation "any more than the Cattle & horses of the North?" And if slaves do have political value, then, logically, shouldn't they have some rights or inputs or protections within the political system? But the point of the debate, at least from the slaveholder's perspective, wasn't to make sense but to protect the institution of slavery by increasing the power of the slaveholding states. And that is exactly what the compromise did. The contemporary Republican Party, in large part because of a process that started with Nixon's Southern Strategy (which involved attracting southern Democrats alienated from the party by the Civil Rights legislation), is now the formal party of racist thought, and now their racist ideas are used as techniques for policy and power.

Why argue that coverage for optional end-of-life counseling sessions constitutes a "death panel" when that is obviously not true? Because it grabs headlines, erodes support for the bill, and draws attention away from the potential benefits of the bill in order to deny President Obama a legislative victory and lay the groundwork for a midterm backlash. More recently Representative Marjorie Taylor Greene claimed that legislation to expand background checks for gun purchases and give federal law enforcement more time to vet gun buyers included a gun registry, even though the legislation actually explicitly excluded one. Republicans act as if increasing the federal deficit is like a gunshot wound when they are arguing against funding social programs because it's an easier argument than arguing some people deserve to starve to death in the richest country in the world. Once again, we find ourselves unable to debate ideas because the ideas do not follow the rules that create debate. You can't debate ideas that aren't interested in being true.

The Tenth Artist

STICK WITH ME through one more thought experiment to try and bring these threads together and a little closer to the world of bookstores.

Imagine that an art gallery invites ten artists to do a joint exhibition. The tenth artist never shows up to set up the exhibition.

The next morning, the gallery owner comes in and all of the paintings in the exhibition have been turned facing the wall. The gallery owner finds a note from the tenth artist that says turning the other paintings around, without getting permission from the other artists, is their contribution to the exhibition.

Obviously, turning the other paintings around is a statement, a personal expression, and perhaps even a critique, and the tenth artist shouldn't go to jail for it. But, though it is the tenth artist's personal expression, it negates the personal expression of all the other artists. It's one thing to say that you believe the back of the canvas has more value than the painting itself, or that the other nine artists do not deserve to be in galleries, but it is another to prevent other people from seeing the paintings.

So what should the gallery owner do? They are responsible for the platform the gallery offers, so they are stewards of the discourse that occurs on the platform. If they think there is value in this particular exchange, they can put in the work needed to make this a meaningful one. They can take photographs of the paintings facing the wall, print them out life-size, turn the paintings the right way, and hang the negations next to their corresponding paintings. That would preserve the image of negation in a way that would carry most, if not all, of the critique inherent in the tenth artist's action, without actually negating the expression of the other artists. It is a creative way to manage the discourse so that the public can interact with all of the expressions and come to their own assessment. (And what the tenth artist should have done to begin with.)

Of course, the gallery owner would be well within their rights to turn all the paintings the right way and tell the tenth artist to fuck right off for being a selfish fucking asshole. Disagreement on a platform takes work to be productive and maybe the gallery owner doesn't want to or doesn't have the time to put that kind of work into their platform at the moment. Given that the tenth artist did not follow the expectations of the exhibition (did not follow the convention of the discourse) and undercut the other artists (actively negated expression in the discourse), why should the gallery owner give the tenth artist a platform?

Now, let's imagine the tenth artist (once again without permission) paints over the other paintings. It is still personal expression, it is still an idea, but once again, it is a negation. The tenth artist's expression erased the expression of the other nine artists. Much like Popper's paradox of tolerance, when negation is allowed to stand on the platform eventually there will only be negation on the platform. To connect back to the nature of compromise, if one expression is a house and the other expression is burning down the house, if the second expression is allowed to stand then there is no more house.

But this expression not only destroys the discourse the gallery owner was trying to create on their platform, it does actual, tangible harm to others. It has cost the nine other artists time, money, and emotional anguish. I think we could all agree they would be well within their rights to sue the tenth artist. I imagine the gallery owner would also be able to sue as they would lose all the potential revenue from selling those paintings. If you were another gallery owner, would you work with the tenth artist? What if the tenth artist claimed they had a right to your platform because their personal expression might be constitutionally protected? What if the tenth artist argued the discourse is only legitimate when he, um, excuse me, when *they* have the right to destroy it?

Now imagine that the tenth artist (again without permission) replaced the descriptions of the paintings with misleading, inaccurate, or deceitful descriptions. You can still see the paintings, but the viewers will interact with them in ways the other artists never intended. This act isn't a complete negation of discourse, but, by preventing the viewers from interacting with the works as they were intended, the discourse has been damaged. To put this another way, honest discourse cannot happen with dishonest materials.

If you were a gallery owner, would you give your platform to the tenth artist? If you know they will undercut the ability of those who actually want to have a discourse from expressing themselves, or will derail the discourse through dishonesty, or might actually do real harm to those others trying to participate? If you would not give the tenth artist a platform in your gallery, why should the New York Times give a platform to climate change deniers? White suprem-acists want to erase the expression of people of color, so why should they be allowed on our platforms? Misogynists want to erase the expression of women, so why should they be allowed on our platforms? All supremacist and phobic ideologies have costumed their ideas in the diction of sci-ence, parading bullshit around (even contradictory bull-shit) as justification for their ideas, so why should we give a platform to someone who bases their conclusions on IQ testing or argues for gay conversion therapy?

Obviously, having a book on your shelves doesn't erase all of the others or somehow prevent a customer from pull-ing others off the shelf, but shelf space is limited. Every book on your shelves is taking the place of another book that could be there. The same goes for display space, which is even more limited. The issue of display space was a major challenge when Porter Square Books was deciding how to handle the controversy around Jeanine Cummins's *American Dirt*. Many members of the staff and management wanted to act on the critique from Mexican and Mexi-can-American critics who argued that *American Dirt* is a racist book, inaccurately portraying Mexico, Mexican cul-ture, and the asylum crisis at our southern border in ways that damaged the discourse around the issue. Others felt that Cummins had been successful in her stated goals, or, at the very least, that altering our decision around displaying the book in response to those critiques infringed on Cum-mins's free expression and/or wasn't the type of judgement we were supposed to make. In the end, we compromised, displaying it on the bestsellers display where it could not really be replaced by another title, but not displaying it in other displays, like the new fiction display, where its space could be given to another book. In other words, beyond the damage done in the wider world, there is an opportunity cost when bookstores choose to stock certain books, just like there is an opportunity cost when the *New York Times* runs a column by a climate change denier or something like Tom Cotton's incendiary piece "Send in the Troops," which argued for military intervention in BLM protests.

Bookstores might be insulated from most of the negating forces in our discourse, and do not have the same moral obligation to vet specific ideas the way the *New York Times* does, but that does not excuse us for supporting those forces on our platform. Much of this essay is written in anticipation of counterarguments, so I feel like I need to make a stronger argument about why bookstores should care about shit that doesn't happen in bookstores, but at the same time, I think Kayla Chadwick phrases it perfectly: "I don't know how to explain to you that should care about other people." Just because you live in a brick house doesn't mean you get to be friends with arsonists.

3.

Exclusion is Part of Inclusion

WHAT YOU HAVE on your shelves is a statement of what you value, just like every book a publisher publishes is a statement of what they value. There is only so much control over how readers and customers interpret that valuation.

What does it feel like for a person of color to walk into a bookstore and see a copy of Sean Hannity's latest book? Is the first thing they see "a commitment to free expression" or "an acceptance of White supremacy"? Do they see "giving space to opinions you disagree with" or "more concerned about an angry old White dude's anger than your fear"? Do they see "This one copy represents a limited platform" or "We're cool with making money off racism"? There are other actions you can take that might earn you the benefit of the doubt from these customers, but even considering the fundamental lack of control one has over how other people interpret one's decisions, regardless of how you frame it, regardless of your specific valuation of the title, when you have a book by a White supremacist on your shelves you are saying "I believe this book has enough value of some kind to justify its author and publisher making money from sales of it at my bookstore." It says "I value the potential sales of the book more than I fear the consequences of these ideas or the author's actions."

What about when someone who is not cisgendered and/or straight sees a book by or celebrating Mike Pence? Pence supports conversion therapy, which is child abuse, his homophobia contributed to an HIV outbreak in Indiana by disrupting a clean needle program, his wife works at a school that excludes homosexuals, and he continually supported Donald Trump through all of his crimes, including declining to support use of the Twenty-fifth Amendment to remove Trump after the insurrection. What does someone of Mexican, South American, or Latin American heritage see when they see *The Art of the Deal* (how many bookstores brought this back into stock when Trump announced he was running for president?) or any of the many books that supported him? Do they think "Well, it's important to include both sides," or do they think "This fucker would have put my children in a cage?" Muslims? People who come from the places Trump called "shithole countries?" Sexual assault survivors? I don't know the answer to these questions and I don't know how many other booksellers do either, because I have not seen these questions asked.

In *Making Spaces Safer: A Guide to Giving Harassment the Boot Wherever You Work, Play, and Gather*, Shawna Potter argues, "[y]ou have to think both holistically and specifically. For instance, don't overlook the little things that make up the overall feel of your space. Don't give a pass to discriminatory statements, art, or 'jokes' on event flyers, tip jars, or band merchandise."[1] One could argue that a single book on the shelf doesn't contribute much to the "overall feel of your space," at least not the way a poster in a music venue would, but faced-out books and displays certainly do. One might argue that even then, the occasional display doesn't mean a whole lot, but as Potter says, "each instance [of harassment] matters, because they add up."[2] Furthermore, they can act as reminders of and potential triggers of past harassment. Seeing a picture of Sean Hannity on the cover of his displayed or faced-out book is not an act of racist harassment, but it can certainly remind people of past acts of racist harassment and it certainly undercuts any goal the store might have of being a refuge for members of their community. Furthermore, "[a] key component of discrimination in our culture is that it minimizes

---

1 Shawna Potter, *Making Spaces Safer: A Guide to Giving Harassment the Boot Wherever You Work, Play, and Gather* (Chico, CA: AK Press, 2019), 25-6.
2 Ibid., 4.

the very real suffering of marginalized people," so be very careful before you argue that something that happens in or is a part of your space is "not that bad" to make sure you have truly examined the act or situation from the perspective of those who might feel hurt by it and factor in how this moment might fit in with a lifetime of accumulated moments. Finally, Potter is very clear about how the idea of "safer spaces" is not supposed to be used. "[I]t's important to point out that, as I use the term, a 'safer space' is not one free of challenging ideas or different opinions. It's not about avoiding exposure to people who are different from you."[3] Potter is speaking primarily from and to the music industry, but I think her ideas are applicable to all managed public and semi-public spaces, including bookstores. As with posters, merch, and other visible aspects of bars and music halls, the books we choose to stock contribute to how safe or unsafe our space feels.

In conversations with booksellers, I've heard it argued that booksellers have an obligation to withhold judgement, that it is not really our job to tell people whether a book is "good" or not, and that it is a violation of our social contract to pass any kind of judgement on books or judge people based on what books they buy. I absolutely agree with the latter idea and very broadly—and when phrased in certain ways—agree with the idea that booksellers should not dictate which books are "good." But I don't really see why choosing not to stock a book because it is written by a White supremacist is fundamentally different from all of the other reasons we have to not stock a book. A customer will have to ask for it at the desk if it's a publisher we don't get good terms from, or if it's about a non-local

---

3 Ibid., 11

sports team, or if the book has gone out of print, like the Dr Seuss books that were pulled by his estate because they contained racist images, or any of the dozens of different reasons why a specific book might not be on the shelves at a particular time. It is also somewhat difficult to hear a principle of non-judgement from an industry that judged and shamed romance readers and writers for decades.

The fact that the Republican Party and much of mainstream conservative media has collapsed into blatant and aggressive White supremacy, xenophobia, misogyny, and fascism, and that much of publishing treats them as if this is acceptable, is their fucking mistake, not yours. Trump being president does not make his ideas worth your shelf space. Fox News getting ratings does not make the ideas of its pundits worth your shelf space. Just because the Republican Party is the largest conservative party in America does not make their ideas worth your shelf space.

Curation is Not Censorship

IN THE SAME way that we know that "free speech absolutism" doesn't exist, we also know exactly what censorship is. Censorship is the suppression or prohibition of speech, communication, or other information on the basis that such material is considered objectionable, harmful, sensitive, or inconvenient. Censorship is what happens when the government bans books, movies, or other media and punishes the production, distribution, or ownership of that media. As private businesses, bookstores are under no obligation to carry any book they don't want to for any reason. And we know this because many bookstores specialize. Primarily carry books by authors of color and authors from marginalized communities? Not censoring White authors. Only carry Sci Fi, Fantasy, Mystery, Romance, Cookbooks, Nonfiction, Poetry? Not censoring other genres. Only carry books by Christian publishers? Not censoring other publishers. Only carry books by authors whose first name is "Jonathan?" Probably not a very good bookstore, but still, not censorship. Nothing a bookstore has the actual power to do is censorship. Whether argued in good faith or bad, with real critical thought behind it or lazy point-scoring, arguing whether a bookstore is censoring a book or author is a waste of time.

As part of those conversations around displaying *American Dirt*, I heard it argued that choosing not to display the book in all of the displays it might fit in "stifled" the free speech of the author. Displays are not an expression of accessibility but of amplification. The book and the ideas and speech it contains will still be accessible whether it is on display, on the shelf, or needs to be special-ordered. Putting it on display simply amplifies it and extends its reach. Furthermore, newspapers, journals, and magazines choose which books to amplify by choosing whether or not to review them or cover them in some other way. Book section editors and book reviewers are not accused of "stifling" free speech when they exercise their editorial discretion by not covering, and thus, not amplifying, a book.

Bookstores are platforms. By carrying, displaying, and special-ordering books, the ideas contained within them are provided with an audience. That platform can be pretty large (stacks on the table, face-outs on the shelves, staff picks, shelf-talkers, events, and promotion on social media), relatively small (a copy on the shelves), or essentially nonexistent (special-ordering books not carried, books listed on industry-wide databases), but as private businesses bookstores have the right to decide which ideas get to use their platforms and which ideas don't, which books they will try to create sales for by putting them in front of customers, which few thousands of books out of the hundreds of thousands published every year will be right at hand. I mean, that is one way to describe the "curation" that Ryan L Rafaelli identified as one of the key components of the independent bookstore resurgence. A bookstore without curation isn't a bookstore, it's a warehouse.

What You Don't Like But Still Stock

WHENEVER CONCERNS ABOUT giving a platform to White supremacists and other demonstrably dangerous ideologies are brought up, someone inevitably argues that bookstores have a responsibility to open discourse and that means bookstores have a responsibility to carry books expressing ideas the booksellers personally disagree with. This point has come up in several conversations I've had and I struggled to articulate this idea in the moment, but "disagreement" isn't the issue. "Destructiveness" is. Whether I, personally, agree with an idea or not is almost beside the point if it is hurting other people. Furthermore, I, personally, have never argued and have never seen or heard anyone argue that bookstores shouldn't carry books with conflicting opinions, or that they should only carry books whose ideas the booksellers agree with. This response seems to be directed at general assumptions about "Social Justice Warriors," "wokeness," or "cancel culture," instead of any actual argument being made. But even then, disagreeing with the ideas expressed in a book doesn't require you to stock it. Just because an idea or a person conflicts with your ideas does not mean productive discourse will come from interacting with that idea or person. And just because a book exists, it does not mean that including it in your platform makes your platform open and inclusive. You are not obligated to keep a bookseller on staff who does no real work for the store. So why should you be obligated to keep ideas on your platform that do no real work for the discourse?

What Can Independent Bookstores Do in the Space They Occupy

INDEPENDENT BOOKSTORES OCCUPY a strange and diffi-cult space in the defense of our national discourse in the age of Trump (an era which is going to outlast him). On the one hand, independent bookstores are respected institu-tions in their communities. We are drivers of the national literary conversation. Individuals and communities look to us for guidance on what to read, which, at least for read-ers, isn't that far removed from looking to us for guidance on how to be. But we are also a tiny fraction of the book industry. For all of our influence, both short and long term, on which books are talked about and which books sell, we actually sell surprisingly few books. Even if every independent bookstore in the country banded together to take some action, in strictly economic terms, it wouldn't amount to a whole lot. The Big 5 publishers would blink, maybe issue a statement, sure, but quickly move on with their publishing plans. Of course, we can't band together to take such actions because, and you'll want to be sitting down for this, antitrust laws make it illegal for bookstores (who are legally competitors) to take many kinds of group action.

Perhaps the most obvious technique is to refuse to sell books that damage our discourse in the ways described above. But no buyer can read every book their store carries. No bookseller can fact-check every assertion and track down every source in every work that claims to be a work of history. We can't vet every book of political nonfiction to make sure it isn't just a collection of racist dog whistles, conspiracy theories, and White grievance. Nor can booksellers hunt down the identity of every author to make sure they aren't Nazis or abusers or TERFs. So when St. Martin's Press tells us that *Killing Lincoln* by Bill O'Reilly is a work of history, we kinda have to believe them.

Or do we?

For me, there is a pretty simple solution. In this political moment, if the author was racist and fascist enough to self-identify as Republican when Donald Trump was party leader, they are racist and fascist enough to be excluded from your platform. If they are racist and fascist enough to be Fox News contributors, they are racist and fascist enough to be excluded from your platform. Will that miss the Gavin McInneses and Richard Spencers of the world? Maybe, but we can't let perfection be the enemy of the good. If we remove nine out of ten White supremacists from our platform, that still counts.

On Bookstores and Bakeries

I'VE HEARD THE argument from a number of different people that if we use our morals to influence our business decisions we're no different from the bakers who refused to make wedding cakes for gay weddings. They used their morals to guide their business decisions and we all condemned it as an act of discrimination. Therefore, if we use our morals to guide our business decisions, we are also committing acts of discrimination.

But there is a big difference between refusing to bake a wedding cake for a gay couple and refusing to stock a book by an author you believe is advancing the cause of White supremacy.

First, gay people don't hurt other people by being gay, but White supremacists (misogynists, xenophobes, homo/transphobes) do. The bakers will claim they are hurt by gay people getting married, but they are wrong. The actions of gayness are not destructive. The actions of White supremacy are. A bookstore that chooses not to work with a racist organization or facilitate the bulk purchase of a racist book by a known racist, identifies a set of actions that are doing actual harm to real people and then refuses to support that set of actions.

Second, and more important for this specific distinction, we are not refusing to serve customers because of who they are. Maybe a bakery doesn't have, I don't know, red velvet cake for some reason. They are not discriminating against you if they won't sell you a red velvet cake, even if you really want a red velvet cake. But if they sell wedding cake and they refuse to sell you a wedding cake because it would be used in a gay wedding, they are discriminating against you. A White supremacist (assuming they aren't doing anything to make staff or other customers feel unsafe) will be able to buy any books we stock from us. Any books we sell. We are not restricting access to our general services and space or choosing to sell some books to some people but not to others. Deciding what to sell is different from deciding who to serve. Refusing to be a revenue stream for White supremacists is different from refusing to sell the books you do have to certain identities.

Customers Are Not the Only People in Your Store

OUR CONVERSATION AROUND curation almost always focuses (somewhat reasonably) on how customers will interact with our stock. But customers are not the only people in our stores. Booksellers (obviously) interact with our selection as well and what that selection says about the values and priorities of our stores. Why would a non-White person take a low-paying, emotionally, intellectually, and physically demanding job that also requires them to sell books by White supremacists? What does it feel like to pour yourself into reading and handselling and event introductions and social media and everything else that booksellers do to make bookstores successful and have someone above you in the organization tell you a person who denies your humanity deserves a presence in your space? What does it feel like to be told Sean Hannity has more of a right to be heard than you have a right to feel safe?

At the very least, have the discussion within your store. Find out what all your booksellers think about the issue. How does the presence of certain books on the shelves impact them? Do any of those books make them uncomfortable? What does it feel like for them to sell one of these books? If they had ultimate power, what would the shelves look like? Though we focus on how customers feel when they are in our stores, we shouldn't neglect how our booksellers feel when they are in our stores. If we want our staffs to look like the real world, if we want booksellers of color, booksellers across the gender spectrum, booksellers with a range of abilities and challenges, both visible and invisible, we need to at least ask them what it feels like to sell books by people who deny their humanity. Another one of those free speech bon mots goes *you have the right to swing your fist until it hits my nose*. If someone on your staff feels like they are getting punched, you owe it to them as human beings and you owe it to yourself as a responsible business owner who relies on the skills and expertise of your staff to at least have the conversation.

Also a Business Decision

WHO IS GOING to actually help keep you open in the long term: the customers and readers who live in your community and seek refuge and resources in your stacks, who see you as something more than a store, who appreciate how being in your store makes them feel, who engage with you in actual conversations on social media, who have made you a part of their lives in big and small ways; or the asshole who complains because you haven't stacked Hannity (or whoever their favorite right-wing pundit is) high enough? What about the provocateur who manipulates controversy for publicity? What about the right-wing group looking to funnel money to a politician they like by bulk purchasing their book?

Who would show up if the store had a fire or was damaged by some natural disaster? Who would show up if one of your booksellers had a health crisis and needed help paying medical bills? Who would pick up a mass market every now and then during a recession because, even though they don't have much money, it is important to them to keep you in their lives? Who would donate to a GoFund-Me? Who would counter-protest in your favor? The people who tweet back and forth with you over the years or the rando who pops into your mentions to say "Ever hear of free speech?"

In short, who is more likely to give you the money you need to stay in business? Customers who have become invested in you as an aspect of their community (both physical and digital) because of the content of your character or those swooping in for one book, one bulk purchase, one event, one tactical display of outrage? From a business standpoint, is it worth risking the former to accommodate the latter?

Furthermore, many, if not most, independent bookstores have decided not to stock books published by Amazon. I remember the discussion around whether or not indie bookstores should carry Penny Marshall's memoir and do not remember any significant concern over the possibility that we might be infringing on the First Amendment rights of Penny Marshall or Amazon as a publisher by declining to stock the book. It's usually framed as rational self-interest. Amazon is a direct and active threat to our businesses and therefore we have decided not to provide a platform for authors that chose to publish with them or become a revenue stream for the company, regardless of the content of the books themselves. Why is that fundamentally different from choosing not to provide a platform or revenue stream to people whose actions are a direct and active threat to human lives?

More Than Negating the Negaters

THROUGH STAFF PICKS, shelf-talkers, displays, events, recommendations, conversations with readers, and on all of our platforms both physical and digital, booksellers should advocate for marginalized voices and communities, center own voices, guide readers to the books and authors that will help them grow and develop as readers, take risks to bring attention to books that might make some readers uncomfortable, use books to show how big the world is, be willing to lose the occasional sale because you have been honest with your readers about a book or an author, respect your readers' intelligence in what books you talk about and how you talk about them, and talk back to publishers and other media in ways that develop and support that vital national discourse. Every shift, every single shift, at an independent bookstore is an opportunity for antifascist, antiracist, anti-supremacist, and anti-misogynist advocacy. What a privilege that is.

Here's a few examples of the kinds of advocacy that we've done at Porter Square Books. In response to the controversy over *American Dirt*, we included a bookmark in every copy in the store that highlighted books by Mexican and Mexican-American authors, fiction and nonfiction, that dealt with the asylum crisis at the US/Mexico border. We created similar bookmarks highlighting books by trans authors to display with JK Rowling's books after she started consistently making transphobic statements. Inspired by Roxane Gay, we also created an event series called Be the Change. Be the Change found authors writing about social, political, and economic issues important to our community and paired them with local nonprofits working directly on those issues, often inviting representatives from the organization to present as part of the event. A percentage of all sales during the event were donated to that organization. These are relatively simple, relatively easy ways to raise up marginalized voices while leading customers to books they might not have encountered otherwise and supporting the conversation around social, economic, and political policy in our community.

Does that opportunity for advocacy mean we can't help readers find fluff? Goof around on social media? Tweet puns at each other? Talk about movies and sports and music? Of course not. Being a reader, being a human, includes goofy shit and bookstores should include that. In many ways, independent brick-and-mortar bookstores are important because they are one of the few public spaces left in contemporary American capitalism that allows us to express and engage in such a wide range of what makes us human.

4.

What Should Bookstores Do?

1. Refuse to stock books written by Republican politicians, members of the Trump administration, and Fox News contributors, and communicate that refusal to publishers. Refuse to host events for them, staff conferences or other off-site events, or facilitate bulk purchases.

2. Refuse to include Republican politicians, members of the Trump administration, and Fox News contributors in na-

tional or regional publicity like the Indie Next List and regional catalogs, and communicate that refusal to publishers.

3. Be active and intentional in your support of antiracist, antifascist, marginalized, and own voices with your staff picks, events, social media, in-store displays, handselling, and other publicity, marketing, and promotions.

Space for Disagreement

CREATING A SPACE for productive discourse between opposing ideas doesn't just happen. Simply having books with conflicting ideologies (with each other and with the general values of your staff and community) doesn't mean you're creating a meaningful exchange of ideas. Work needs to be done for people to feel safe enough to hear critique, to confront their own biases, to cope with learning that something they long held to be true might, in fact, be false. Even an event, or an event series, isn't necessarily going to create that space without preparation and active (and experienced) moderation.

Porter Square Books held an event with Jean Trounstine, author of *Boy with a Knife: A Story of Murder, Remorse, and a Prisoner's Fight for Justice*. *Boy with a Knife* uses the case of Karter Kane Reed, who committed murder when he was sixteen, to argue for criminal justice reform around the sentencing of juvenile criminals as adults. The family and friends of the victim organized a protest at the event. Before the event, one of the store's managers spoke separately with the author and the protestors, essentially acting as a negotiator, listening to what both sides needed to feel heard and safe. They agreed that the protestors would stay outside, chanting and holding signs, during the event, but that they would not try to prevent anyone from coming in. After the event, a small number of representatives would have the opportunity to converse with the author. The event went off without a hitch. After the audience filed out, the manager led the representatives of the protestors into the store and stayed in the space during the conversation. It was, I would say, a very successful event and exchange.

But that successful exchange didn't just happen. It took work on the store's part, both before and during the event, to create a space where people could exchange opposing ideas. Furthermore, the manager who handled this situation is a fifty-something-year-old White man and a former lawyer. He looks like a figure of authority and he knows the language of both authority and negotiation. It wasn't easy for him, but his identity and his education made this difficult situation a lot easier than it might have been. If you don't know how your bookstore could create that space for disagreement, if you don't have the time, energy, or expertise to create that space, or the resources to hire someone who can, well, maybe your bookstore actually isn't the right public space for those types of conversations.

Taking Our Eye Off the Ball

HONESTLY, IN THE time it takes me to write this sentence, the whole context for this piece could change. Who knows what's going to happen between when I finish this and someone reads it? Maybe Trump is in jail. Maybe the Republican Party is in absolute shambles. Maybe we have a Green New Deal. Maybe we have Medicare for all. Let's

get totally wild and say that maybe we start paying repa-
rations. Maybe White supremacist and fascist ideas don't
seem like a threat. Historically, progress has often been
followed by setbacks. Reconstruction was followed by Jim
Crow. The Civil Rights Movement was followed by the
War on Drugs, welfare reform, criminal justice reform,
and other explicitly or indirectly segregationist policies to
create the system that Michelle Alexander calls "the New
Jim Crow." President Barack Obama was followed by President Donald Trump.

White supremacy is persistent. We are here now because too many people, too many White people, saw a few
big wins as proof of final victory. We took our eye off the
ball. We must be as persistent as White supremacy. We
must remember that our society didn't get this way by ac-
cident, that we don't "just happen" to live in a White supremacist state, and we won't "just grow out of it." We got
here actively and so cannot be passive if we want to move
forward.

The Least We Can Do

FOR ALL THE importance, for all the significance, for all
the literal lives on the line as we fight for justice, I'm struck
by how little, ultimately, I'm asking of my colleagues. For
many of us, I'm not even asking you to lose that many sales.
A couple dozen over the course of the year. The occasional
hundred-copy bulk purchase. The occasional fifty-copy
event. A loss, sure, but nothing that would stand out in a
year-end statement. The work of advocacy doesn't really
need to be new work. You just might need to redirect,
refocus, and be more intentional with the staff picks you

already write, the handselling you already do, and events you already host. Maybe you need to do a little work to find books or authors outside your comfort zone, but there are plenty of resources out there for that. Depending on your store, you might want to develop a script for booksellers to use if customers ask about books you don't stock (though, honestly, I'd just say "We're out of stock right now"). You might also want to develop a process for handling belligerent customers, but you should probably have one anyway.

I don't know if, at this stage, deplatforming White supremacists and fascists from indie bookstores will have much of an impact, especially in the context of shit like, you know, violent insurrections. For all of our influence, for all of our value to our communities, the big publishers (who are the problem) wouldn't be impacted much at all. But I'd rather fight and lose than not fight at all. If, as a bookseller, I can't push the needle towards justice, at least I won't be holding it back. Maybe, ultimately, all of these efforts end at our doors and all we've done is create spaces slightly freer of White supremacy. That feels worth it to me. That is important to me. To me, that seems like the least we can do.

JOSH COOK is a bookseller at Porter Square Books in Cambridge, Massachusetts, where he has worked since 2004. He is also author of the critically acclaimed postmodern detective novel *An Exaggerated Murder* and his fiction, criticism, and poetry have appeared in numerous leading literary publications. He grew up in Lewiston, Maine and lives in Somerville, Massachusetts.

DEDICATION
To the Founders of Porter Square Books,
who hired me and supported me early in my career,
the managers and other libromancers at Porter Square Books,
who continue to make this job so fun and rewarding,
and my friends and comrades in books,
working too hard and getting paid too little
to bring books to the people.

The Least We Can Do by Josh Cook was first printed in an edition of
1000 copies for Independent Bookstore Day 2021.

Readied for the press by Daniel Wells
Cover designed by Michel Vrana

Published with the generous assistance of Ontario Creates

ONTARIO | ONTARIO
CREATES | CRÉATIF

ISBN 978-1-77196-465-4

PRINTED AND BOUND IN CANADA